RAVENS
PROBLEM SOLVERS

KATIE
LAJINESS

AWESOME ANIMAL
POWERS

Big Buddy Books

An Imprint of Abdo Publishing
abdopublishing.com

abdopublishing.com

Published by Abdo Publishing, a division of ABDO, PO Box 398166, Minneapolis, Minnesota 55439.
Copyright © 2019 by Abdo Consulting Group, Inc. International copyrights reserved in all countries.
No part of this book may be reproduced in any form without written permission from the publisher.
Big Buddy Books™ is a trademark and logo of Abdo Publishing.

Printed in the United States of America, North Mankato, Minnesota.
052018
092018

THIS BOOK CONTAINS
RECYCLED MATERIALS

Cover Photo: John Dreyer/Getty Images.
Interior Photos: Al Tielemans/AP Images (p. 29); blickwinkel/Alamy Stock Photo (p. 7); Elizabeth
    Candy / EyeEm/Getty Images (p. 9); Esther Kok / EyeEm/Getty Images (p. 15); iStock/Getty
    Images (p. 30); Kaapro/Getty Images (p. 11); Lara Montagnac / EyeEm/Getty Images (p. 19);
    Laszlo Szirtesi/Getty Images (p. 17); Markus Spiering / EyeEm/Getty Images (p. 21); Michael
    Macdonald / EyeEm/Getty Images (p. 23); MorenaKi/Getty Images (p. 25); Pat Gaines/Getty
    Images (p. 5); Vassiliy Vishnevskiy/Getty Images (p. 27).

Coordinating Series Editor: Tamara L. Britton
Contributing Editor: Jill Roesler
Graphic Design: Jenny Christensen, Erika Weldon

Library of Congress Control Number: 2017961381

Publisher's Cataloging-in-Publication Data

Names: Lajiness, Katie, author.
Title: Ravens: Problem solvers / by Katie Lajiness.
Other titles: Problem solvers
Description: Minneapolis, Minnesota : Abdo Publishing, 2019. | Series: Awesome animal
    powers | Includes online resources and index.
Identifiers: ISBN 9781532115035 (lib.bdg.) | ISBN 9781532155758 (ebook)
Subjects: LCSH: Ravens--Juvenile literature. | Ravens--Behavior--Juvenile literature. |
    Animal intelligence--Juvenile literature. | Problem solving--Juvenile literature.
Classification: DDC 598.864--dc23

CONTENTS

THE RAVEN

The world is full of awesome, powerful animals. Ravens (ray-VEHNS) live throughout North America. Many know them as very smart birds that can **solve** difficult problems. And, they can **mimic** the sounds of other types of birds and humans.

Many people confuse ravens with crows. Ravens are larger birds. And, they do not travel in large groups.

BOLD BODIES

The largest of the songbirds, ravens weigh about three pounds (1 kg). They can be up to 27 inches (69 cm) long. These birds have strong bills and longer tail feathers. Their feathers are completely black with a blue, green, or purple shine.

DID YOU KNOW?

A raven's spread wings can be 46 to 56 inches (117 to 142 cm) long!

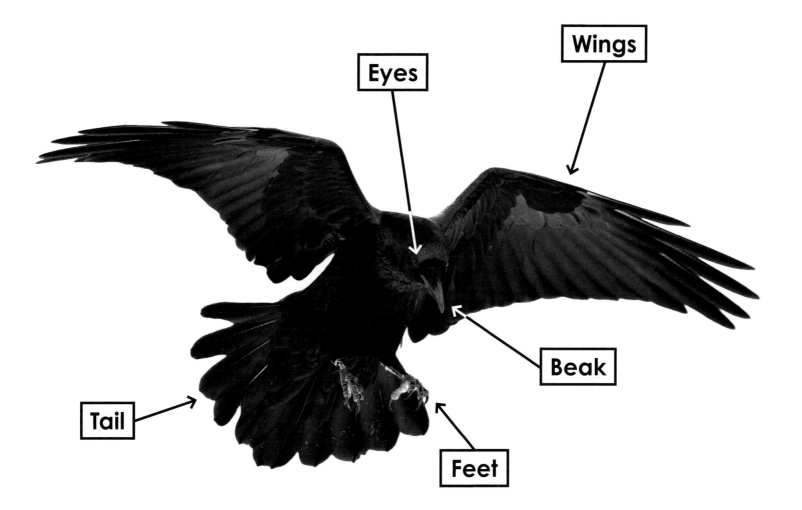

THAT'S AWESOME!

Ravens are very smart. Like humans, they can **solve** puzzles. Scientists have done many studies on ravens. They have shown ravens are as smart as chimpanzees and dolphins.

These smart birds push rocks onto paths to scare strangers away from their nests. They have also taken fish from fishermen's lines.

Ravens are able to think many steps ahead to solve a problem. They can choose which tools will help them catch tastier foods.

Ravens have awesome animal powers. In the wild, they **mimic** birdcalls to lead wolves and foxes to their **prey**. Then ravens let larger animals kill the prey. This makes the meat easy for ravens to eat later.

Ravens trick other birds by pretending to hide food in one place. While the other bird looks for the food, the raven actually hides it someplace else.

WHERE IN THE

Ravens live throughout North America except for the southeastern United States. They also live in Asia, North Africa, and Europe.

These birds can live in nearly any **climate**. They like to live in forests and cities. But they can also live in deserts, **tundras**, and along sea coasts.

WORLD?

= WHERE RAVENS LIVE

ARCTIC OCEAN

North America

Europe

Asia

PACIFIC OCEAN

NORTH ATLANTIC OCEAN

Africa

South America

PACIFIC OCEAN

SOUTH ATLANTIC OCEAN

INDIAN OCEAN

Australia

N
W E
S

DAILY LIFE

Most ravens spend time alone or with one other raven. But sometimes they team up to hunt for food.

Ravens are called **scavengers**. So they search for **carrion** that another animal has already killed. Sometimes they store food to eat later.

Ravens are protective of their territory and food.

Female ravens spend a lot of time building their nests. They build these homes on cliffs, in trees, on telephone poles, or in bridges.

The outer part of the nest is made of sticks, earth, and grass. Then, these clever birds line the inside with soft grasses, wool, hair, or moss. Building a nest takes between nine days and two weeks.

Ravens can mimic at least 30 different voices such as hailing, warning, threatening, taunting, and cheering.

A RAVEN'S LIFE

Ravens are quite playful. When flying, they glide through the air. Some ravens will drop objects from up high. Then they quickly dive to catch them.

These smart birds like to play pranks on humans and other animals. They have even been seen unzipping zippers to get at food!

In 1845, writer Edgar Allan Poe wrote a famous poem called "The Raven."

These birds are usually awake during the day to look for food. Food can be hard to find in the winter. So, ravens will store it during the spring and summer. Or they will open trash cans to look for food.

The raven is famous in Norwegian stories. The god Odin had two ravens that flew around the world each day. These birds then told Odin all they had seen.

FAVORITE FOODS

Ravens will eat almost anything. They like to eat mice, rabbits, insects, and frogs. But they also eat **carrion** from animals that other **predators** have killed. When there is no meat, these birds will also eat fruit or grains.

Young ravens are fed insects. As they grow older, they begin eating what their parents eat.

Some ravens will steal foods from picnic tables!

BIRTH

A female raven lays three to seven spotted eggs. These eggs can be green or blue with purple or brown spots. The mother sits on the eggs to keep them warm. The eggs hatch 20 to 25 days later.

Many believe raven couples stay together for life.

DEVELOPMENT

Once raven eggs hatch, both parents feed the young. The parents crush insects for food. As the young birds grow, they begin to eat more foods. The parents then feed them the meat from small animals.

Young ravens can fly at about six weeks old. But the parents care for them for another five months. This way, the young can learn life skills and grow stronger.

Baby ravens are not born black. Instead, the babies have gray down feathers.

FUTURE

Since the 1960s, raven **populations** have grown across North America. Today, there are about 20 million ravens worldwide. Most people expect that these smart birds will continue to **thrive** for many years.

Many sports teams use ravens as their mascots. The Baltimore Ravens, a professional football team, is named after the bird.

FAST FACTS

ANIMAL TYPE: Bird

SIZE: 22 to 27 inches (56 to 69 cm)

WEIGHT: About three pounds (1.3 kg)

HABITAT: Forests, beaches, mountains, deserts, grasslands, and cities

DIET: Small animals, carrion, insects, berries, and grains

AWESOME ANIMAL POWER:
Ravens are very smart birds that can solve problems and use tools.